NATURAL
DISASTERS
AN IMAGINATION LIBRARY SERIES

VOLCANOES

by Victor Gentle and Janet Perry

Gareth Stevens Publishing
A WORLD ALMANAC EDUCATION GROUP COMPANY

S

Please visit our web site at: www.garethstevens.com
For a free color catalog describing Gareth Stevens' list of high-quality books and multimedia programs, call 1-800-542-2595 (USA) or 1-800-461-9120 (Canada). Gareth Stevens Publishing's Fax: (414) 332-3567.

Library of Congress Cataloging-in-Publication Data

Gentle, Victor.
    Volcanoes / by Victor Gentle and Janet Perry.
       p. cm. — (Natural disasters: an imagination library series)
    Includes bibliographical references and index.
    ISBN 0-8368-2836-4 (lib. bdg.)
    1. Volcanoes—Juvenile literature. [1. Volcanoes.]
    I. Perry, Janet, 1960- II. Title. III. Series.
    QE521.G43 2001
    551.21—dc21   00-051624

First published in 2001 by
Gareth Stevens Publishing
A World Almanac Education Group Company
330 West Olive Street, Suite 100
Milwaukee, WI 53212 USA

Text: Victor Gentle and Janet Perry
Page layout: Victor Gentle, Janet Perry, and Joel Bucaro
Cover design: Joel Bucaro
Series editors: Mary Dykstra, Katherine Meitner
Picture researcher: Diane Laska-Swanke

Photo credits: Cover © AP/Wide World Photos; p. 5 © David Lea/Living Letters Productions, from the video *Montserrat's Andesite Volcano*, see p. 22; pp. 7, 21 © Roger Rossmeyer/CORBIS; p. 9 © North Carolina Museum of Art/CORBIS; p. 11 Joel Bucaro/© Gareth Stevens, Inc., 2001; p. 13 © D. Cavagnaro/Visuals Unlimited; p. 15 © CORBIS; p. 17 © Dave B. Fleetham/Visuals Unlimited; p. 19 © Bettmann/Corbis

Printed in the United States of America

1 2 3 4 5 6 7 8 9 05 04 03 02 01

Front cover: *February 2000: Mayon volcano in the Philippines erupts. Forty-thousand people living in the area were moved to safer grounds during a lull in the series of eruptions.*

TABLE OF CONTENTS

Words that appear in the glossary are printed in **boldface** type the first time they occur in the text.

A Mountain Blows

"Soufriere Hills volcano is **active** and will erupt again." This warning was made in 1987 by volcano scientists at work on the tiny Caribbean island of Montserrat.

Eight years later in July 1995, the volcano began a series of eruptions. By February 1997, the volcano looked so dangerous that everyone in the area was warned to leave. Many people moved away. Some left the island altogether. About eighty people stayed in the danger zone. They had gotten used to the rumblings and the eruptions, and they weren't afraid.

Then, in June 1997, the volcano blew. Within minutes, whole villages were buried by a searing-hot stream of rock and ash. Nineteen people died.

Soufriere Hills volcano has been active ever since it sprang to life again in 1995. Here, it is erupting, billowing hot ash and smoke into the sky above Montserrat.

BURYING WHOLE VILLAGES

In some parts of the world, huge amounts of rock deep in the ground heat up so much that the rock melts. When molten, or melted, rock is underground, we call it **magma**.

A volcano occurs when magma pushes, or erupts, through the Earth's surface. Often, a mountain forms where this happens. The volcanic mountain is made of rocks, ash, and **lava** that explode into the air or gush out of the volcano during an eruption.

A volcanic eruption can be quite mild. Or it can be very strong and blow a whole mountain to pieces. An explosion like this would blot out the Sun with dust and bury the land nearby in falling rocks, hot ash, and lava. Thousands of people, animals, and plants might die.

A river of red-hot lava flows from Mount Etna in Sicily, Italy, during an eruption in January 1992. The volcano has erupted frequently over thousands of years.

Mysterious Volcanoes

What causes volcanoes? What melts the rock in the first place? Why does magma come to the surface? Why do some volcanoes explode, but others flow gently? Why are volcanoes *where* they are? Can we predict when a volcano is going to erupt?

People have tried to answer these questions for thousands of years. Today, most **geologists** hold different beliefs than those held by geologists just fifty years ago.

Why do we think today's beliefs are better? It is because today's beliefs seem to explain more about volcanic activity. However, fifty years from now, scientists may have completely different thoughts that provide an even better explanation of volcanoes.

A painting by P. J. Volaire of an eruption of Mount Vesuvius in the 1700s. For thousands of years, people have puzzled over what causes these devastating fireworks.

FROM CORE TO CRUST

The planet we live on is shaped, more or less, like a ball. The distance from the center of the Earth to the surface is about 3,960 miles (6,380 kilometers).

Many scientists believe that Earth's center is a large globe (the **core**). This globe contains an inner core that is mainly solid iron. Around the inner core is the outer core: a thick layer of molten metal, mostly nickel and iron. Earth's core is surrounded by very hot rock, from about 1,800 miles (2,900 km) deep and nearly reaching the Earth's surface. This rock, called the **mantle**, is under huge pressure.

Above the mantle is a thin, rocky **crust**. Earth's crust is thickest under the continents, averaging about 28 miles (45 km). Under the oceans, it is much thinner, averaging only about 5 miles (8 km).

A cutaway diagram of the layers of rock and metal inside our planet. The solid outer part of the mantle and the rocky crust together are called the lithosphere.

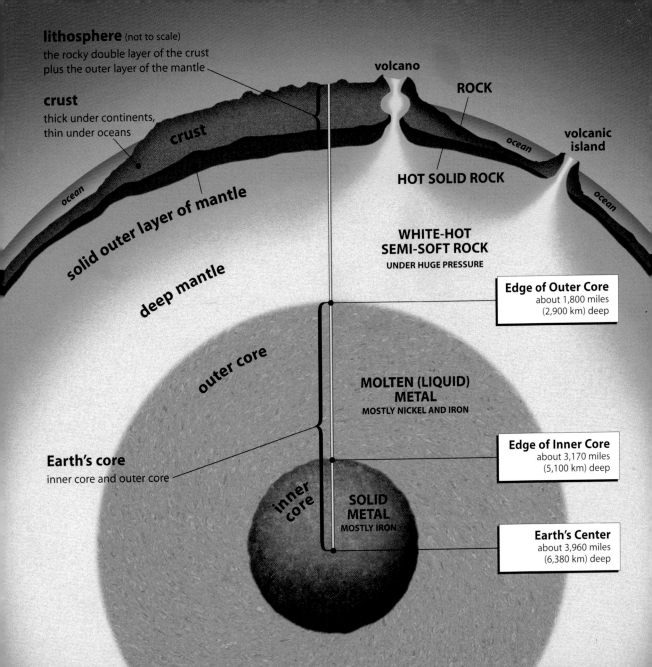

lithosphere (not to scale)
the rocky double layer of the crust
plus the outer layer of the mantle

crust
thick under continents,
thin under oceans

volcano

ROCK

crust

ocean

volcanic
island

ocean

HOT SOLID ROCK

solid outer layer of mantle

ocean

**WHITE-HOT
SEMI-SOFT ROCK**
UNDER HUGE PRESSURE

deep mantle

Edge of Outer Core
about 1,800 miles
(2,900 km) deep

outer core

**MOLTEN (LIQUID)
METAL**
MOSTLY NICKEL AND IRON

Edge of Inner Core
about 3,170 miles
(5,100 km) deep

Earth's core
inner core and outer core

inner
core

**SOLID
METAL**
MOSTLY IRON

Earth's Center
about 3,960 miles
(6,380 km) deep

SLAMMING SLABS

Mantle rock has two main layers. Both are very hot. The outer layer is solid. The deeper mantle layer is not molten like magma. Instead, it is more like very thick taffy. It flows — very, very slowly. Over *long* periods of time, the deeper mantle acts like a thick, slow-boiling jam.

Continents and ocean floors are made up of huge pieces of Earth's crust and the solid mantle rock layer joined together. These double-thick slabs, called **plates**, float on the hot, taffy-like part of the mantle. Slowly, over thousands of years, they slam into each other, pushed by currents in the lower mantle. They grind against each other or rise up and over one another. One plate can force its neighbor down into the soft mantle below.

When crust or mantle rock melts underground, it is called magma. When magma reaches the surface, it is called lava. Here, molten lava hardens into solid rock lava as it cools.

SUBDUCTION ZONE BLASTS

A **subduction zone** is formed when one plate forces another downward. When this happens, a large amount of energy is released as heat. Deep down, where it is already hot, this extra heat melts the rock, water, and other materials. This is one way that huge underground pools of red-hot magma are made.

Magma is lighter than the surrounding rock, so it bubbles its way upward. Wherever it finds weakness in the rock above, it pushes and melts its way through. Earthquakes sometimes weaken the rocks above, guiding the magma to where it forces its way up into the air (or the sea) above.

The famous Mount St. Helens volcano sits on a big subduction zone in the northwestern United States.

Triggered by an earthquake, Mount St. Helens erupts on May 18, 1980, killing more than fifty people and devastating 250 square miles (650 square km).

HOT SPOT VOLCANOES

Some volcanoes are found in the middle of plates, often a long, long way from the active edges.

The Hawaiian Islands volcanoes are like this. One volcano after another has built up from the Pacific Ocean floor in the same spot. At the same time, the Pacific plate has been moving. Over thousands of years, a chain of volcanic islands has formed.

Each volcano has grown, then slowly moved northwest by about 3.4 inches (8.6 centimeters) every year for the last 43 million years. As the volcanoes move away from their "birthplace," or **hot spot**, they become less and less active.

Lava from the Kilauea volcano meets the sea. Kilauea is a very active hot spot volcano, the closest on land to the hot spot that created the Hawaiian Islands chain.

OTHER VOLCANOES

Volcanoes can be found over hot spots and where plates grind alongside or crunch into each other. They also occur where plates are moving apart. Most of these areas are found under oceans and are called **mid-ocean rifts**.

Where undersea plates are moving apart, lines of volcanoes ooze thick, dark lava, called **basalt**, into the water. This basalt provides new plate material to replace plate material that is "lost" in subduction zones.

The theory of how and why all these huge plates move is called plate tectonics. *Tectonics* means "the science of how things are built."

Smoke and steam billow from a new volcano vent, or opening, in 1965. A new island is born off Iceland, a large volcanic island sitting on both a mid-ocean rift and a hot spot!

THE LONG AND SHORT OF IT

The theory of plate tectonics seems like a good *long-term* explanation for volcanic activity (and for earthquakes, too) over millions of years.

However, it is also important to be able to predict if a nearby volcano is going to erupt today, next week, or next month. Are there signals that an eruption is about to take place? How big will the eruption be? Are lives in danger? What can we do to save people, animals, and property?

Most active volcanoes have teams of scientists studying them, trying to find answers to these *short-term* questions. As scientists get better at predicting the short-term behavior of volcanoes, people may listen more carefully to their warnings.

Volcano scientists from the Hawaii Volcano Observatory take measurements, standing on a recent flow of lava hot enough in places to melt their shoes.

MORE TO READ AND VIEW

Books (Nonfiction)   *Earthquakes (Natural Disasters).* Victor Gentle and Janet Perry
    (Gareth Stevens)
Mount St. Helens: The Eruption and Recovery of a Volcano.
    Rob Carson (Sasquatch)
Volcano and Earthquake. Susanna Van Rose (Dorling Kindersley)
Volcanoes. Allison Lassieur (Capstone)
Volcanoes (Associated Press Library of Disasters). Robin Doak (Grolier)
Volcanoes: Earth's Inner Fire. Sally M. Walker (Carolrhoda)
World Almanac for Kids. Elaine Israel (World Almanac Books)

Books (Activity)   *I'll Know What to Do: A Kid's Guide to Natural Disasters.*
    Bonnie S. Mark and Aviva Layton (Magination)
The Young Geographer Investigates Volcanoes and Earthquakes.
    Terry Jennings (Oxford)

Books (Fiction)   *Vacation Under the Volcano.* Mary Pope Osborne (Random Library)
The Volcano Disaster. Peg Kehret (Minstrel)

Videos (Fiction)   *Volcano.* (Twentieth Century Fox)

Videos (Nonfiction)   *Deadly Shadow of Vesuvius.* (WGBH/NOVA)
Eyewitness: Volcano. (Dorling Kindersley)
Hawaii Born of Fire. (WGBH/NOVA)
In the Path of Killer Volcano. (WGBH/NOVA)
*Montserrat's Andesite Volcano.** (Living Letters Productions)
National Geographic's Volcano: Nature's Inferno. (National Geographic)
*Volcano Island.** (Living Letters Productions)
Volcanoes of the Deep. (WGBH/NOVA)

* These videos document the Soufriere Hills eruptions mentioned on page 4 and can
be obtained through www.priceofparadise.com.

22

WEB SITES

If you have your own computer and Internet access, great! If not, most libraries have Internet access. The Internet changes every day, and web sites come and go. We believe the sites we recommend here are likely to last and give the best and most appropriate links for our readers to pursue their interest in volcanoes, earthquakes, tsunamis, plate tectonics, and geoscience.

www.ajkids.com

Ask Jeeves Kids. This is a great research tool.
Some questions to try out in Ask Jeeves Kids:
Are there different kinds of volcanoes?
What other planets in our solar system have volcanoes?

You can also just type in words and phrases with "?" at the end, for example:
Shield volcano?
Lava flow?
Mid-ocean rift?
Geoscience?
Plate tectonics?

volcano.und.edu

Volcano World. A great site with special features on recent eruptions of volcanoes, on Mount St. Helens, and other topics. There are lots of pictures, both in video and plain snapshots. Their kids' section (**volcano.und.edu/vwdocs/kids/kids.html**) is full of awesome volcano information and things to do: visit an online gallery, get school project ideas, play games, learn volcano legends, go on virtual field trips, link to other schools' volcano home pages, and take a quiz!

www.ngdc.noaa.gov/seg/hazard/hazards. shtml/

Natural Hazards Databases — a U.S. Government site. In addition to offering an amazing photo gallery (click on "slide sets") of earthquakes, tsunamis, volcanoes, and other natural hazards (and the debris that they leave behind), this site features a series of kids' quizzes on hazards ranging from volcanoes and earthquakes to wildfires and tsunamis.

www.hsus.org/disaster/index.html

A visit to the Humane Society of the United States site will help you learn how to create a disaster action plan for everyone in your family — including your pets. If you have a pet that isn't listed in this site, you can easily link up to other sites (The American Red Cross, Horse Review) that have excellent suggestions for handling your pets in an emergency.

GLOSSARY

You can find these words on the pages listed. Reading a word in a sentence helps you understand it even better.

active — erupting regularly 4, 16, 20

basalt (buh-SALT) — a dark, volcanic rock 18

core — the sphere of hot metal, both solid and molten, at the center of Earth 10

crust — the thin outer layer of Earth 10, 12

geologists (jee-AH-luh-jists) — scientists who study the Earth, its structure, and the way it works 8

hot spot — a fixed place on our planet where magma forces its way to the surface, regardless of the movement of plates 16, 18

lava — molten or solidified rock that has come out of a volcano 6, 12, 18, 20

magma — molten rock beneath the surface of the land or the ocean floor 6, 12, 14

mantle — the 1,730-mile- (2,800-km-) thick rocky layer between the Earth's thin crust and the Earth's core 10, 12

mid-ocean rifts (MID oh-shen RIFTS) — regions of the ocean floor where plates are moving apart as new plate material is made from magma from below 18

plate — a very large slab made up of crust and an outer solid layer of the earth's mantle 12, 14, 16, 18

subduction zone (sub-DUCK-shen zone) — an area where one plate is being pushed beneath another 14, 18

INDEX